A
Literature Unit
for

Rifles for Watie

by Harold Keith

Written by Michael Shepherd

Edited by Patricia L. Miriani

Illustrated by Sue Fullam and Keith Vasconcelles

Teacher Created Materials, Inc.

P.O. Box 1214

Huntington Beach, CA 92647

©1992 Teacher Created Materials, Inc.

Made in U.S.A.

ISBN 1-55734-413-2

Table of Contents

Introduction

A good book can touch our lives like a good friend. Within its pages are words and characters that can inspire us to achieve our highest ideals. We can turn to it for companionship, recreation, comfort, and guidance. It also gives us a cherished story to hold in our hearts forever.

In *Literature Units*, great care has been taken to select books that are sure to become good friends!

Teachers who use this unit will find the following features to supplement their own valuable ideas.

- Sample Lesson Plans

- Pre-Reading Activities

- A Bibliographical Sketch and Picture of the Author

- A Book Summary

- Vocabulary Lists and Suggested Vocabulary Activities

- Chapters grouped for study, with each section including:
    - *quizzes*
    - *hands-on projects*
    - *cooperative learning activities*
    - *cross-curriculum connections*
    - *extensions into the reader's own life*

- Post-reading Activities

- Book Report Ideas

- Research Ideas

- A Culminating Activity

- Three Different Options for Unit Tests

- Bibliography

- Answer Key

We are confident that this unit will be a valuable addition to your planning, and hope that as you use our ideas, your students will increase the circle of "friends" that they can have in books!

Sample Lesson Plan

Each of the lessons suggested below can take from one to several days to complete.

LESSON 1

- Introduce and complete some or all of the pre-reading activities on page 5.
- Read "About the Author" with your students. (page 6)
- Introduce the vocabulary list for Section 1. (page 8)
- Ask students to find possible definitions for these words.

LESSON 2

- Read chapters 1 through 5. As you read, place the vocabulary words in the context of the story and discuss their meanings.
- Choose a vocabulary activity. (page 9)
- Make battle flags. (page 11)
- Act out a scene from the novel. (page 12)
- Discuss and research Civil War history. (page 13)
- Discuss students' attitudes toward becoming a soldier. (page 14)
- Administer the Section 1 quiz. (page 10).
- Introduce the vocabulary list for Section 2. (page 8)
- Ask students to find definitions for these words.

LESSON 3

- Read chapters 6 through 10. Place the vocabulary words in context and discuss their meanings.
- Choose a vocabulary activity. (page 9)
- Make corn dodgers or corn puffs. (page 17)
- Draw a battle map. (page 18)
- Discuss Cherokee Indians. (page 19)
- Analyze relationships between friends and enemies. (page 20)
- Administer Section 2 quiz. (page 16)
- Introduce the vocabulary list for Section 3. (page 8)
- Ask students to find definitions for these words.

LESSON 4

- Read chapters 11 through 15. Place the vocabulary words in context and discuss their meanings.
- Select a vocabulary activity. (page 9)
- Make a soldier's scrapbook. (page 22)
- Play a Civil War game. (page 23)
- Add up the miles Jeff Bussey marches. (page 24)

- Learn how to move the injured. (page 25)
- Administer Section 3 quiz. (page 21)
- Introduce the vocabulary list for Section 4. (page 18)
- Ask students to find definitions for these words.

LESSON 5

- Read chapters 16 through 20. Place the vocabulary words in context and discuss their meanings.
- Choose a vocabulary activity. (page 9)
- Sing a Civil War song. (page 27)
- Play Twenty Questions. (page 28)
- Research and discuss the invention of new weapons. (page 29)
- Discuss the conflict between spying and friendship. (page 30)
- Administer Section 4 quiz. (page 26)
- Introduce the vocabulary list for Section 5. (page 8)
- Ask students to find definitions for these words.

LESSON 6

- Read chapters 21 through 25. Place the vocabulary words in context and discuss their meaning.
- Choose a vocabulary activity. (page 9)
- Draw details on a uniform. (page 32)
- Describe the good qualities of the rebels. (page 33)
- Translate dialect into standard English. (page 34)
- Determine your ideal husband/wife. (page 35)
- Administer Section 5 quiz. (page 31)

LESSON 7

- Discuss any questions your students have about the story. (page 36)
- Assign book report and research projects. (pages 37 and 38)
- Begin work on culminating activity. (pages 39 through 41)

LESSON 8

- Administer Unit Tests: #1, #2, and/or #3. (page 42, 43, and 44)
- Discuss the test answers and possibilities.
- Discuss the students' enjoyment of the book.
- Provide a list of related reading for your students. (page 45)

4

Before the Book

Before you begin reading *Rifles for Watie* with your students, do some pre-reading activities to stimulate interest and enhance comprehension. Here are some activities that might work well in your class.

1. Predict what the story might be about by hearing the title.

2. Predict what the story might be about by looking at the cover illustration.

3. Discuss other books about soldiers and war that students may have heard about or read.

4. Answer these questions:

    • Are you interested in:

        — The American Civil War?

        — Romance?

        — Stories about young people proving themselves?

        — Battles, spies, and adventures?

    • Would you ever:

        — Volunteer to fight in a war?

        — Show kindness to your wartime enemies?

        — Volunteer to spy on the enemy?

        — Fall in love with someone on the enemy side?

    • Have you ever wondered what the Civil War was really like for the soldiers fighting in it?

5. Work in groups to make your own wartime scrapbook. *(Include World War II, Korea, Vietnam, Persian Gulf. See page 22 for suggestions.)*

About the Author

Harold Verne Keith was born April 8, 1903, in Lambert, Oklahoma Territory, to Malcolm Arrowwood (a grain buyer) and Arlyn (Kee) Keith. Harold loved history, and began writing because of his interest in history. "I was lucky to have really fine history teachers," said Mr. Keith. One was Dr. E. E. Dale at the University of Oklahoma. Keith received both bachelor's and master's degrees from the University of Oklahoma, where he did extensive research on the Civil War and the involvement of Indians in the war.

From 1930 to 1968, Mr. Keith served as sports publicity director for the University of Oklahoma. In 1936, he published *Boy's Life of Will Rogers*, a biography of the well-known humorist from his home state. In 1940, his *Sports and Games* became a Literary Guild selection. He began writing children's fiction with a regional flavor in 1949 with *Shotgun Shaw*, followed by *A Pair of Captains*, 1951; *Rifles for Watie*, 1957; and *Komantcia*, 1965, a novel about a Spanish boy, Pedro, who is kidnapped by the Comanche Indians. *The Runt of Roger's School* was published in 1971. *Susy's Scoundrel* (1974) describes the relationship between a wild coyote and an Oklahoma Amish girl who adopts him. Mr. Keith has also contributed sports fiction stories to *American Boy* and *Bluebook*. He has written for the *Saturday Evening Post* and *Esquire*.

Harold Keith starts writing early in the morning. He works for four hours before going for a run with friends and returning to work in his library for about two more hours. Now in his late 80's, Mr. Keith is working on a sequel to *Komantcia*.

Mr. Keith has won many awards. In 1958, he received the John Newbery Medal for the most distinguished contribution to literature for American children for *Rifles for Watie*. A former steeplechase winner in the Penn Relays as an undergraduate, Harold Keith remained a distance runner in his later years and, recently, broke the U.S. Master's Association three-mile record for men over seventy.

(Information for this biography came from a telephone interview with Mr. Keith on March 16, 1992 and from *Contemporary Authors, New Revision Series*, Volume 2, 1981)

Rifles for Watie

by Harold Keith

(Harper & Row, 1987)

Jeff Bussey, sixteen, volunteers for the Union Army after Confederate raiders continually threaten his family's Kansas farm. He finds himself marching for hours, drilling with a rifle and coping with harsh treatment by a regular army officer, Captain Asa Clardy. Clardy resents Jeff's name, Jefferson Davis Bussey, because Jefferson Davis is the president of the Confederate states the Union is fighting.

Jeff sees his friends die in battle and in army hospitals. He tries to be helpful even to those residents of Oklahoma and Arkansas sympathetic to the southern cause, and falls in love with a rebel girl, Lucy Washbourne. Jeff inherits a new pet, a dog, when its former owner, a Confederate officer, falls in battle.

Jeff tries to help Lucy when her brother, a spy for Cherokee rebel leader Stand Watie, is executed by Union soldiers. Jeff pays for the body to be sent home to the Washbournes. Later, Jeff himself is chosen to spy on the Confederates and finds himself posing as a rebel in Watie's Cherokee Mounted Rifles. Jeff respects the Southerners so much that he is tempted to stay on with Watie. But when Jeff witnesses Captain Clardy selling Spencer repeating rifles to the Confederates, his sense of duty calls him to deliver this information to Union officers at Ft. Gibson.

After many close calls, escapes, and pursuit by rebels, Jeff makes it back to the Union fort. Jeff makes it home to Kansas and renews his courtship of Lucy Washbourne. She has promised to wait for him in spite of his faithfulness to the Union cause.

7

Vocabulary Lists

On this page are vocabulary lists which correspond to each sectional grouping of chapters. Vocabulary activity ideas can be found on page 9 of this book.

SECTION 1
Chapters 1-5

Jefferson Davis	Abraham Lincoln
Union	bushwacker
slur	desertion
furlough	incredulously
military	impertinent
volunteer	inspection
insolently	reluctant
pungent	vindictive

SECTION 2
Chapters 6-10

prudent	amputation
bivouac	chloroform
cicadas	ambulance
pickets	appreciative
bayonets	confiscation
foraging	stridently
disenchanted	crestfallen
epaulets	jocularly

SECTION 3
Chapters 11-15

Cherokee	hardtack
Yankee	fieldwork
sauciest	cavalry
belligerent	ravenously
brogans	illuminated
recruit	brandishing
indignantly	execrable
perplexed	

SECTION 4
Chapters 16-20

swarthy	seminary
astonishment	gargoyle
enthralled	ghostlike
Gettysburg	scrutinized
Vicksburg	diagnosis
scout	unintelligible
spasmodically	carbine
provost	

SECTION 5
Chapters 21-25

gingerbread	red-handed	contraband
federal	exultantly	cupola
repeating rifle	clandestine	sardonic
accompanying	commissary	monotonous
enlistment	expectancy	

8

Vocabulary Activity Ideas

You can help your students learn and retain the vocabulary in *Rifles for Watie* by providing them with interesting vocabulary activities. Here are a few ideas to try.

❑ People of all ages like to make and solve puzzles. Ask your students to make their own **Crossword Puzzles** or **Wordsearch Puzzles** using the vocabulary words from the story.

❑ Challenge your students to a **Vocabulary Bee**. This is similar to a spelling bee, but in addition to spelling each word correctly, the game participants must correctly define the words as well.

❑ Play **Vocabulary Concentration**. The goal of this game is to match vocabulary words with their definitions. Divide the class into groups of 2-5 students. Have students make two sets of cards the same size and color. On one set have them write the vocabulary words. On the second set have them write the definitions. All cards are mixed together and placed face down on a table. A player picks two cards. If the pair matches the word with its definition, the player keeps the cards and takes another turn. If the cards don't match, they are returned face down to the table, and another player takes a turn. Players must concentrate to remember the locations of words and their definitions. The game continues until all matches have been made. This is an activity for free exploration time.

❑ Have your students practice their writing skills by creating sentences and paragraphs in which multiple vocabulary words are used correctly. Ask them to share their **Power Vocabulary** sentences and paragraphs with the class.

❑ Ask your students to create paragraphs which use the vocabulary words to present **History Lessons** that relate to the time period or historical events mentioned in the story.

❑ Challenge your students to use a specific vocabulary word from the story at least **10 Times In One Day**. They must keep a record of when, how, and why the word was used!

❑ As a group activity, have students work together to create an **Illustrated Dictionary** of the vocabulary words.

❑ Play **20 Questions** with the entire class. In this game, one student selects a vocabulary word and gives clues about this word, one by one, until someone in the class can guess the word.

❑ Play **Vocabulary Charades**. In this game, vocabulary words are acted out.

You probably have many more ideas to add to this list. Try them! See if experiencing vocabulary on a personal level increases your students' vocabulary interest and retention.

Quiz Time

1. On the back of this paper, write a one paragraph summary of the major events in each chapter of this section. Then complete the rest of the questions on this page.

2. Describe the conflict in Linn County, Kansas.

     _____

     _____

3. What does Jeff decide to do after the bushwhackers come to his home? Why?

     _____

     _____

4. Explain the problem Jeff has with his first and middle names.

     _____

     _____

5. Why does Captain Clardy not get along with Jeff?

     _____

     _____

6. David Gardner doesn't like the army. What does David do? How does Jeff try to help?

     _____

     _____

7. What do you think David Gardner's mother should have done when she saw David?

     _____

     _____

8. Describe Jeff's punishment by Clardy.

     _____

     _____

9. How do the soldiers sneak watermelons into camp?

     _____

     _____

10. What would you do if you had to confront someone like Captain Clardy? Write your answer on the back of this page.

Battle Flags

Jeff Bussey finds himself caught in the historic American conflict of the nineteenth century, the Civil War. North and South fought from 1861 to 1865 over the issue of slavery and the right to secede from the Union. Thousands of Americans died as families and states were divided and Americans fought against other Americans. Each side had a banner. Both banners changed their looks during the course of the war.

The original Confederate flag, adopted in 1861, had seven stars to represent the seven seceding states.

This flag looked too much like the U.S. flag, so troops carried a battle flag. In 1863, a new flag was adopted, but it looked too much like a flag of truce, so in 1865 a red bar was added to the flag.

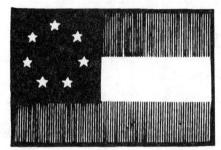

Original Confederate Flag (1861)

Battle Flag

1863 Flag

1865 Flag

The U.S. flag also underwent changes. Abraham Lincoln refused to have the stars representing the southern states removed. For the first three months of the war the flag had 33 stars, then 34 stars until 1863, when it had 35 stars until the end of the war.

In the army, each regiment has its own flag. These flags are assigned by the Department of Heraldry. A regiment's flag can be compared to a family's coat of arms. It tells some history of the regiment. It could include anything from pictures of landforms to represent the geographic location, to the names of battles the regiment has been involved in.

It's your turn to design a flag. It could be a regiment flag for either regiment Jeff Bussey was involved with. Be sure to include symbols which would represent the men and their backgrounds.

You may wish to design a flag that the Confederates might have adopted if they had won the war. You could design a new U.S. flag of the future. Be creative. Have there been more states added? What about space colonies? Or, you may wish to design a flag representing your school or classroom.

Act It Out!

Jefferson Davis Bussey, "Jeff," has a problem with his name. When he joins the Union army, Jefferson Davis is the name of the president of the breakaway Confederacy which the Union is fighting against.

It all comes to a head when Captain Asa Clardy gets angry at Jeff because the young recruit doesn't understand that "Fix bayonets" means to put the bayonet on the end of the rifle. When Clardy learns Jeff's name, he tells the boy to change it.

> *"Jeff felt the hair rise on the back of his neck. He neither liked the remark nor the man that delivered it.*
>
> *'Sir,' he said, looking the captain fearlessly in the eye and continuing to speak loudly, 'I won't change it. My father gave me that name. He knew Jefferson Davis before the Mexican War. He fought in Jefferson Davis' regiment at the Battle of Buena Vista.' "*

Clardy punishes Jeff by assigning him to wash pots, peel potatoes, and empty swill after spending a full day marching and drilling.

In a group of 2-3 students, act out the drill-field scene or another scene from *Rifles for Watie*. You may wish to change the scene and add a little military humor in one of the following ways:

- Think of another controversial name, for example "Abraham Lincoln" or "Cary A. Rifle." Have the men sound off during roll call as the captain gets angrier and angrier.

- Create a dialogue between Jeff and another soldier while they peel potatoes. They can discuss the army, Captain Clardy, and how to avoid getting into trouble with the officers.

- Have Captain Clardy visit Jeff while he washes pots. "You missed a spot," says the captain. How does Jeff respond?

- Act out the scene in which Jeff is emptying waste water and Captain Clardy, thinking it is soup, tastes it, spits it out, and has a few choice words for Jeff.

- Create a scene where Jeff is told by Clardy that he must darn his socks.

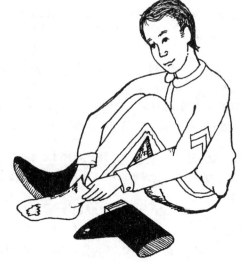

Civil War Time Line

Many American boys Jeff's age (16) and under fought in the Civil War. Slaves, free Blacks, and Native Americans were involved in the conflict. Americans from all parts of the country, including the west, struggled for things they believed in.

Why did the Civil War happen? Use an encyclopedia or other reference books to make a time line of the major events before and during the war. Be sure to include the Kansas-Nebraska Act and Bleeding Kansas to understand Jeff's home state situation. Write the letter of each event in the box next to the correct year on the time line.

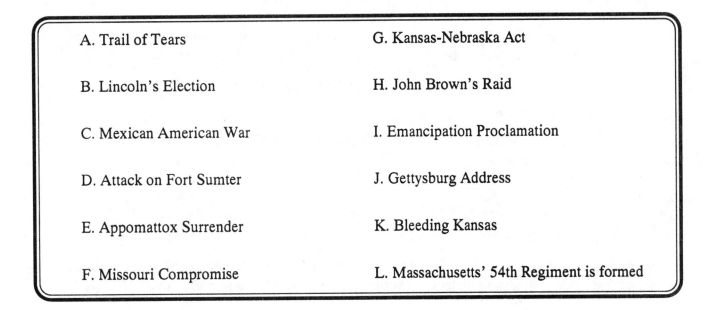

A. Trail of Tears   G. Kansas-Nebraska Act

B. Lincoln's Election   H. John Brown's Raid

C. Mexican American War   I. Emancipation Proclamation

D. Attack on Fort Sumter   J. Gettysburg Address

E. Appomattox Surrender   K. Bleeding Kansas

F. Missouri Compromise   L. Massachusetts' 54th Regiment is formed

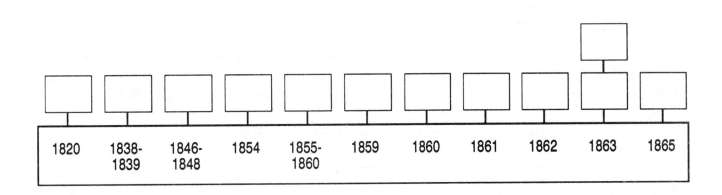

Find out more about the roles of slaves and free Blacks in the Civil War. An excellent source is *Undying Glory* by Clinton Cox. (Scholastic, 1991)

Volunteers for America

When Southern bushwhackers continually harassed the Bussey family, Jeff Bussey volunteered to be a part of the solution by joining the Union Army. Today, you might need to volunteer to solve some problem in your neighborhood, city, state, or nation. In the next few pages, you will become a problem solver, a volunteer for America!

You will need to follow these steps:

       * Define the problem.

       * Plan a solution.

       * Implement your solution.

What problem would you like to help solve? Volunteer to solve a problem you really want to deal with! Here are a few things other people have defined as problems that may help you make up your mind:

adult illiteracy	child abuse
school drop-out rate	litter
drug abuse	moral/spiritual decline
water pollution	crime
air pollution	poverty
noise pollution	loneliness
homelessness	

Choose one of the problems from the list above, or come up with one of your own, and state it in a complete sentence. Define the problem in your local situation and be a specific as you possibly can.

_____

_____

_____

Now that you have defined your problem, list five possible ways that you could help solve the problem.

1. _____

2. _____

3. _____

4. _____

5. _____

Volunteers for America *(cont.)*

List five resources that could help you solve the problem (friends, clubs, churches, agencies, donors, etc.). Be specific. Tell how they could help.

_____

_____

_____

_____

_____

_____

_____

_____

_____

How will you know when the problem is solved? How will you measure your success?

_____

_____

Now that you have selected the problem you want to work on and have a plan for solving it, begin to implement your solution. On a calendar or diary, list and date the action you have taken to solve the problem.

Clean Up Central Park

Sunday	Monday	Tuesday	Wednesday	Thursday	Friday	Saturday
		1	2	*Call volunteers* 3	4	5
6	Meet at 4:30 7	8	Make posters 9	10	11	Clean up litter 12
Separate cans 13	14	Go to recycle center 15	16	Speak at local business 17	18	19
20	21	22	23	24	25	Clean up litter 26
Separate cans 27	28	Go to recycle center 29	Donate money to charity 30			

Quiz Time

1. On the back of this paper, write a one paragraph summary of the major events that happen in each of the chapters in this section. Then complete the rest of the questions on this page.

2. What is Jimmy Lear's problem?

_____

_____

3. What happened when Jeff fired off his gun to clean it?

_____

_____

4. Retell Sparrow's story about Captain Clardy.

_____

_____

5. Why is Jeff disappointed at the Battle of Wilson's Creek?

_____

_____

6. One of Jeff's friends is wounded in battle. What happens to his leg?

_____

_____

7. Describe Jeff's duty after the battle and the new friend he makes.

_____

_____

8. How does Sparrow die?

_____

_____

9. How are rebel families in Missouri punished for their husbands' military service? What does Jeff do for Mrs. McCommas?

_____

_____

10. On the back of this paper, describe the two Cherokee groups found in Oklahoma during the Civil War.

Corn Meals

Jeff and the entire Union Army had to forage for food if they wanted any variety in their diet. One of the few staple items they were issued was corn meal, so they quickly learned a number of ways to fix cornbread.

Try the recipe below or another simple cornpone treat. Can your class members forage for ingredients?

Corn Dodgers

Materials:

mixing bowl

spoon

baking sheet

1 cup (250 mL) stone-ground cornmeal

1 tsp. (5 mL) salt

1 ½ tsp. (7.5 mL) sugar

1 cup (250 mL) boiling water

2 tbls. (30 mL) butter or bacon drippings

1 beaten egg

Directions:

Preheat oven to 400° F (200° C).

Combine stone-ground cornmeal, salt, sugar. Stir in boiling water. Beat in butter or bacon drippings and an egg until blended.

Drop the batter from a spoon onto a greased baking sheet; or dip your hand in cold water, fill it with batter and release the batter "splat" onto the sheet. Bake for 20 minutes.

Corn Puffs

Materials

pan

baking sheet

2 ¼ (560 mL) cups boiling water

1 cup (250 mL) yellow stone-ground cornmeal

1 tablespoon (15 mL) sugar

1 tablespoon (15 mL) salt

2 tablespoons (30 mL) butter

2 eggs, separated

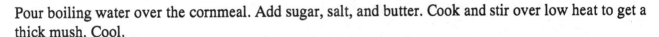

Directions

Preheat oven to 425° F (220° C).

Pour boiling water over the cornmeal. Add sugar, salt, and butter. Cook and stir over low heat to get a thick mush. Cool.

Beat egg whites until stiff. Add egg yolks to cooled mixture and beat in well. Fold in beaten egg whites.

Drop large spoonfuls of batter onto a greased baking sheet. Bake for 20 minutes.

Battle Map

The Civil War in the western United States is not as well-known as the battles in the east where General Robert E. Lee faced General Ulysses S. Grant. But the battles in the west were important because, to win the war, Union forces had to control the Southern supply lines, and ultimately, conquer the rebel states.

Make a large mural map of the United States. This can be done either by tracing a large wall map or by photocopying a small textbook map, transferring the impression onto acetate, and projecting the image with an overhead projector onto mural paper.

On your map, show battles and other major events of the novel and the broader Civil War. On flashcard-size strips, show where Jeff fought and what happened in the battle. Here are some places and events to include:

Wilson's Creek, Missouri: Jeff is called to deliver a message behind the front lines and misses the battle. Ford Ivey's leg is amputated after he is wounded in battle.

Talequah, Oklahoma: Jeff meets Lucy Washbourne.

Rolla, Missouri: Jeff forages for food, helps punish Confederate families but secretly helps Mrs. McCommas.

Linn County, Kansas: Jeff's home, a center for "Bleeding Kansas" struggles between pro and anti-slavery settlers.

Cherokee Nation: Northeastern Oklahoma, around Talequah.

Pheasant Bluff: Battle on the Arkansas River in Eastern Oklahoma.

Boggy Depot, Oklahoma: Town in Southern Oklahoma, Confederate capital of Oklahoma.

Prarie Grove, Arkansas: Here, for the first time, Jeff fights in a Civil War battle.

Red River: Boundary line between Texas and Oklahoma.

Texas Road: Jeff's flight from Boggy Depot to Ft. Gibson paralleled this road.

Rebel Indians?

Stand Watie is the feared Confederate leader who united the Cherokee Indians to fight against the Union. He raids Union supply trains, attacks Union soldiers, and generally allies his tribe with the secessionists.

> *"Jeff had heard of Stand Watie, a warlike Cherokee of mixed blood, who owned slaves and commanded a small, hard-riding rebel cavalry unit that had begun to raid, boldly and sharply, the comfortable homes, fields, and livestock of the Union Indian sympathizers who had not yet left the country. Cherokees, Choctaws, Chickasaws, Seminoles, and Creeks—most of them were now fighting actively with the South."*

Using *Rifles for Watie*, encyclopedias, and other reference books, discover why many Cherokees supported the Confederacy and not the Union during the Civil War.

What did the U.S. Government do to the Cherokees and other tribes in the 1830's?

_____

_____

_____

How did the Cherokees feel about slavery?

_____

_____

_____

Describe the two different groups of Cherokees; the followers of Chief John Ross and the followers of Stand Watie.

_____

_____

_____

Union soldiers "foraged" for food on Cherokee land. Is what they were doing considered stealing? Was this right or wrong? Explain.

_____

_____

_____

Friendly to the Enemy

Union soldiers confiscated livestock from Missouri rebel families to punish them for fighting against the United States. Jeff unenthusiastically participates in the confiscation, but later helps a friendly lady, Mrs. McCommas, by sneaking her cow back to her. He does this by sneaking out at night and bribing the cow lot guard with some of Mrs. McCommas' apple butter and homemade bread. Jeff was genuinely sympathetic to the woman who lost her cow, in spite of the fact that her husband was fighting for the Confederacy.

Consider how you act toward friends and enemies as you answer the following questions:

1. Have you ever done anything to help someone who was your enemy? How did they respond?

    _____

    _____

    _____

    _____

2. Have you ever felt friendlier toward people who were supposed to be your enemies than you felt toward people who (like Captain Clardy) were supposed to be on your side? Explain.

    _____

    _____

    _____

    _____

3. Was Jeff doing the right thing when he returned Mrs. McCommas' cow? Why or why not?

    _____

    _____

    _____

    _____

4. Have you ever done something against the rules but you felt it was the right thing to do? Give details.

    _____

    _____

    _____

    _____

Quiz Time

1. On the back of this paper, write a one paragraph summary of the major events that happen in each of the chapters of this section. Then complete the rest of the questions on this page.

2. Who is Lucy Washbourne? How does Jeff react to seeing her?

_____

_____

3. How do the Washbournes treat Jeff?

_____

_____

4. Describe the battle of Prairie Grove.

_____

_____

5. Who saved Jeff's life?

_____

_____

6. What happened to Jimmy Lear?

_____

_____

7. Why was Jeff's regiment happy to be in Van Buren, Arkansas?

_____

_____

8. How did Jeff help Lucy out of an awkward situation?

_____

_____

9. What happened to the Brandt family? Why?

_____

_____

10. On the back of this paper, describe how you have helped (or been helped) out in a difficult situation.

Soldier's Scrapbook

Jeff has many experiences during his Civil War service. He makes new friends, like Noah Babbit, and sees friends die from wounds suffered in military service. Jeff develops friendships with "enemy" sympathizers and even falls in love with a rebel girl. He collected many memories. What kind of scrapbook might Jeff have made?

You may have a friend or relative who served in one of the U.S. wars: The Gulf War, Panama incursion, Granada invasion, Vietnam, Korea, World War II. Put together a scrapbook of events that occurred during the war. Find photographs, news clippings, letters, and other items that tell the story of the war. If possible, interview your friends on a cassette tape recorder or video camcorder and have them tell about their experiences during the war. If you do not know anyone who has served in a war, you may wish to make up a character and do a fictional interview. Be sure to do research so your information is accurate.

Here are some possible interview questions:

- Where were you stationed?
- What was your rank?
- What were your responsibilities?
- Were you in or near any major battles?
- What was your branch of service?
- Who were your best friends in the military?
- Were you ever wounded?
- What role did women play in the military?
- How did you feel when you returned home?
- Were you drafted or did you volunteer?

- Do you still keep in contact with military buddies?

Scavenger Hunt

Divide the class into groups of two or three. Distribute a scavenger hunt list to each group. Each group will complete a math problem and use classroom and library resources to complete the hunt successfully. When all groups have finished, answers may be shared with the class and written on index cards to be shuffled and reused, along with other questions about the Civil War to play North vs. South. Divide the class into two groups, Union and Confederacy. One member from each team stands as the teacher reads a question. The first player to correctly answer the question earns a point for his or her team. If neither player can answer the question, it is returned to the pile.

Group 1

1. How did the use of repeating rifles change the war?

2. Why was Kansas called "Bleeding Kansas"?

3. Where is the site of the famous July, 1863 battle?

4. In what year did the Civil War begin?

5. Complete the math problem to find out what year Lincoln was reelected. $932 \times 2 =$

Group 2

1. Who was Matthew Brady?

2. What are bounty jumpers?

3. Why did West Virginia split away from Virginia during the Civil War?

4. What is the site of Robert E. Lee's surrender?

5. Complete the math problem to find the year in which the Emancipation Proclamation came into effect.
$(3 \times 6 \times 100) + (7 \times 9)$

Group 3

1. Name the states that fought for the Confederacy.

2. Where did both Ulysses S. Grant and General Robert E. Lee train to become soldiers?

3. Did more soldiers die of hunger, wounds, or disease?

4. In what year did General Lee surrender?

5. Complete the math problem to find out the Confederate population in 1860. (250,000 divided by 10) - 16,000; x 1,000.

Group 4

1. What are ironclads?

2. What was the judge's decision in the Dred Scott case?

3. Who was the president of the Confederacy?

4. Who led the march through Georgia?

5. Complete the math problem to find the number of Union losses at the 2nd Battle of Bull Run.
$(2 \times 7000) + 700 + (6 \times 9)$

Tramp, Tramp, Tramp

Jeff Bussey marched with the Union Army all over Arkansas, Missouri, Oklahoma, and Kansas. He was exhausted and hungry much of the time. How far did he march?

Trace Jeff's route on the map below. Using the scale of miles, estimate how far he walked. Record your results below:

START	STOP	Number of Miles
Linn County	Fort Scott	_____
Fort Scott	Wilson's Creek	_____
Wilson's Creek	Prairie Grove	_____
Prairie Grove	Van Buren	_____
Van Buren	Talequah	_____
Talequah	Fort Gibson	_____
	Total	_____

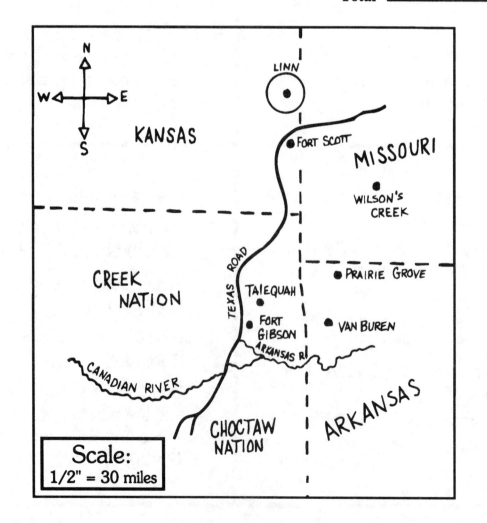

Scale:
1/2" = 30 miles

First Aid

Jeff Bussey and every soldier who has ever been in battle has faced the possibility of death. In *Rifles for Watie*, Jeff watches a friend lose a leg and sees a wounded boy, Jimmy Lear, die in a military hospital at age 15. Jeff manages to get through the war heroically, wins a medal for bravery, and gains friendship, respect, and admiration for an older soldier, Noah Babbit, who saves Jeff's life.

Would you know what to do if someone was seriously injured? The way a person is moved could mean the difference between life or death. Whenever possible, you should wait for an ambulance or other professional assistance. If there is no other option, you should take the following steps in moving a seriously injured person.

- Using whatever is available, try to build a stretcher that will support the person (door, ironing board, table top, blankets, etc.).

  Here are directions for one possible stretcher that may be tried in a classroom. Use two brooms, a blanket, and the steps illustrated below. Use the stretcher to carry a "victim," following the directions below. Be sure to have enough people to safely support the person being carried. This should be done on a gym mat or other soft surface in order to keep the injuries make-believe.

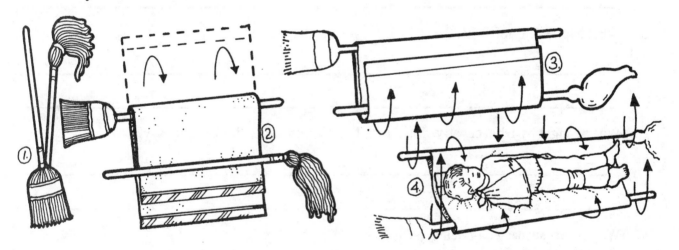

- Place supporting materials around the key areas—head, neck, shoulders, and back. Also support any other injured areas.

- Splint any broken bones or sprains. (Use newspapers, magazines, or anything available.)

- When all areas of the body have been supported, move the person as a single unit, making sure the body does not turn or twist. This should be done with as many people helping as is possible. One person should be above the head, holding it on both sides to make sure it stays straight. Others should be spaced a few inches apart. The person who is holding the head should give the signal to start. At the signal, roll the person onto his or her side and slide the stretcher under the person until it reaches his or her shoulder that is on the ground. Then carefully, in one movement, place the person onto the stretcher.

- Once the person is on the stretcher, use available materials (belts, scarves, clothing, etc.) to tie him or her to the stretcher.

Quiz Time

1. On the back of this paper, write a one paragraph summary of the major events that happen in each of the chapters of this section. Then complete the rest of the questions on this page.

2. What does Jeff do when he finds out that Lee Washbourne has been shot as a spy?

    _____

    _____

3. Why does General Blunt want Jeff to act as a spy?

    _____

    _____

4. How does Jeff return the favor to Noah Babbitt for saving his life?

    _____

    _____

5. What happens to Jeff when he visits Lucy for the third time?

    _____

    _____

6. When caught by rebel cavalry, what does Jeff's companion, Jim Bostick, say?

    _____

    _____

7. Why is Jeff suspected of being a Yankee spy?

    _____

    _____

8. How does Jeff get to know the Jackman family? Where does he go with them?

    _____

    _____

9. Who does Jeff trust to get his message to Fort Gibson?

    _____

    _____

10. On the back of this paper, describe what you would say if an enemy soldier confronted you while you were spying behind his lines.

Sing Me a Song!

Soldiers during the Civil War loved to sing. In _Rifles for Watie_ and in nonfiction accounts of the war, we read about soldiers from opposing armies singing to one another across the battle lines at night as they sat around their campfires. All the tension of battle faded as they broke into their favorite melodies and entertained one another.

Union campfire singers had their favorite, Bill Earle, who sang a beautiful tenor. But there was more than just singing going on when Captain Clardy asked Bill to sing. He was sending a message to the Confederates!

Marching soldiers liked to make up their own parodies of favorite songs. For example, instead of the original "Dixie," which starts "I wish I was in the land of cotton, good times there are not forgotten, look away, look away, look away Dixie land," the Kansas recruits would bellow: "I wish I was in Douglas County, two years up and I had my bounty, look away, look away, look away, Kansas said."

Practice and sing one of the following Civil War tunes individually or as a group. Then try to write your own parody of a popular song.

Dixie

John Brown's Body

Shoo Fly Shoo

Wait for the Wagon

Come Where My Love Lies Dreaming

Tramp, Tramp, Tramp

Pop Goes the Weasel

Lily Dale

Goober Peas

When Johnny Comes Marching Home

Beautiful Dreamer

Shenandoah

Streets of Laredo

Twenty Questions

Jim Bostwick, caught behind enemy lines with Jeff, has to explain quickly who they are. Jim makes up a story about who they are—boys out to join the Confederate cavalry under Stand Watie.

Not satisfied completely with the answer, the rebels are still suspicious of Jim and Jeff, especially when they find Union coffee in Jim's canteen!

Do you know who the characters in the novel really are? What side of the war are they on? Divide your class into three or four groups for a game of Twenty Questions. Each person in a group is assigned a character from the novel. When it is your character's turn, other members of your group will have twenty chances to ask questions that are answerable by "Yes" or "No." As soon as the identity of the person is guessed, try the next character in your group. For example:

1. Is the character male?   (Yes)

2. Is he a Union soldier?   (No)

3. Is he a Confederate soldier?   (Yes)

4. Is Jeff friends with him?   (No)

5. Is he killed in the war?   (Yes)

6. Is it Lee Washbourne?   (Yes)

Here are possible characters:

Jeff Bussey	**Lucy Washbourne**
Noah Babbitt	**Captain Asa Clardy**
Dave Gardner	**Lee Washbourne**
Lieutenant Orff	**Jim Bostwick**
Mrs. Jackman	**Heifer Hobbs**

You may wish to use the names of important people or events of the Civil War. Use reference books or encyclopedias to find information about the following people:

Abraham Lincoln	**Jefferson Davis**
Ulysses S. Grant	**Robert E. Lee**
William T. Sherman	**Stonewall Jackson**
George B. McClellan	**Frederick Douglass**
Clara Barton	**Harriet Tubman**

Inventions

Repeating rifles that fired quickly again and again without reloading were used during the Civil War. They were also used for fighting with Native Americans after the war. With such a weapon, one man could fight off several other men who only held single shot rifles or bows and arrows. If there were equal numbers of men in a battle, but one side had repeating rifles and the other side had single shot firearms, is there any doubt which side would have the advantage?

Again and again throughout history, one group of people has tried to gain the advantage over their enemies by securing superior weapons of war. Research one or more of the following inventions and explain how it gave its owner an advantage over an enemy.

ironclad ships (such as the *Monitor* and *Merrimac*)

submarines

repeating rifles

machine guns

torpedo

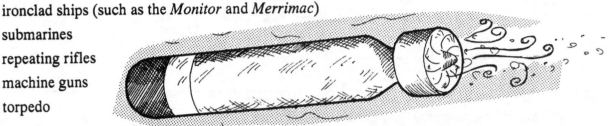

Many other inventions during the late 19th century gave manufacturers an advantage over their competitors, allowing them to produce products more quickly. Research one or more of the following inventions that helped cause the industrial revolution in America.

linotype

monotype

typewriter

vacuum cleaner

steamship

tractor

rubber tires

electric street car

steam engine

web perfecting printing press (Andrew Campbell)

photography

motion pictures

gasoline engine

Bessemer (steel making)

automobile

train

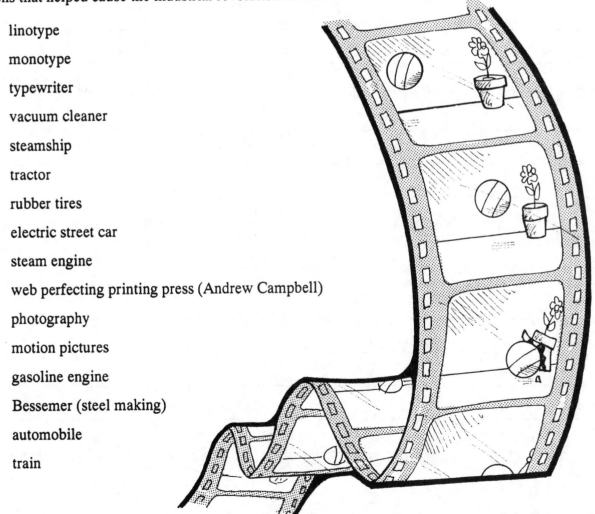

Which Side Are You On?

As a spy behind Confederate lines, Jeff has to get information about the enemy and report it back to General Blunt. Jeff does get information about rebel troop movements and passes it by way of a sympathetic slave who wants to help the Northern army.

In order to accomplish his mission, Jeff has to pretend to be a Southern recruit. He even fights in battle against his own army and saves the life of one of the Confederate cavalrymen who suspects him of spying! Jeff becomes close friends with Heifer Hobbs, the rebel cook, who practically adopts him as a son. When Jeff falls ill, he becomes close friends with a Confederate family, the Jackmans, who take him to Texas with them until he recovers.

Have you ever pretended to be someone you are not? Explain.

_____

_____

Have you ever felt guilty about being friends with someone who is nice to you, when you are really deceiving that person? Describe the situation.

_____

_____

_____

Do you think it is important to show hospitality to people you don't know very well? Why or why not?

_____

_____

A spy risks being shot. What are the risks of lying to someone who thinks you are on their side of a conflict?

_____

_____

When is it O.K. not to tell the truth? Why?

_____

_____

_____

Quiz Time

1. On the back of this page, write a one paragraph summary of the main events that happen in each of the chapters of this section. Then complete the rest of the questions on this page.

2. If the Southern Army acquired a large number of Springfield repeating rifles, how would it affect the war?

   _____

   _____

3. Why does Jeff like the Watie men?

   _____

   _____

4. Is it difficult for Jeff to be a spy? Why or why not?

   _____

   _____

5. What does Jeff find out about Captain Clardy?

   _____

   _____

6. How does Jeff finally get back to his Union regiment?

   _____

   _____

7. What does Jeff tell Lucy before his escape?

   _____

   _____

8. Explain how Jeff gets yet another new pet.

   _____

   _____

9. What does Jeff take home with him from the army?

   _____

   _____

10. On the back of this paper, predict what will happen to Jeff after the war.

It's a Draw!

Below is a picture of Jeff as an infantryman or foot soldier.　However, his uniform is incomplete.　Help Jeff finish his uniform by adding a knapsack, bayonet, canteen, rifle, hat, and boots.　When you have drawn in the items, color his uniform accurately.　You may need to find a picture of a Union soldier in an encyclopedia, a reference book about the Civil War, or a textbook to help complete this assignment.

Tempted to Change Sides

Jeff spies on Watie's Cherokee Mounted Rifles, fights in battles with them, and gets to know and like Southern sympathizers such as the Jackmans, who take care of him when he is sick. Jeff is tempted, because he likes these people and loves Lucy Washbourne, to change sides and stay with the Confederates.

What are the good qualities of the people he is spying on? Work in groups of three or four to describe the traits Jeff sees and admires in the rebels. Then, as a group, come to a decision about what you would have done under the same circumstances.

1. Heifer Hobbs

   _____

   _____

   _____

2. Stand Watie

   _____

   _____

   _____

3. The Jackmans

   _____

   _____

   _____

4. Lucy Washbourne

   _____

   _____

   _____

5. Hooley Pogue

   _____

   _____

   _____

What Did He Say?

In the Southern United States, many people use a regional dialect of English when they speak. They say "y' all" instead of "you all" and "soljuh" for "soldier." Sometimes it can be hard for people from other parts of the country to understand.

Harold Keith, author of *Rifles for Watie*, writes southern and black dialectical speech into the novel. See if you can rewrite some of the statements below using standard English spelling and punctuation.

" 'They built it fifteen years before I was borned. They sho' did do somethin'...It stands theah in the woods apointin' its spire up towards heaven. Evah time I passes it, I feels kinda reverent-like.' "

_____

_____

_____

" 'Y'all can eat with oauh mess heah.' "

_____

" 'Sam, yore addled...What else does the boy have to do today to prove himself to ya—tote cha on his back all the way from Honey Springs to Red Rivah?' "

_____

_____

_____

" 'Hop in theah an' crawl 'tween the covahs.' "

_____

" 'Dat Miss Pat done it again...She nevah gonna leahn to walk graceful, lak a lady.' "

_____

_____

" 'Dey's fixed you a pallet in de back ob one ob de wagons.' "

_____

_____

34

True Love

Jeff Bussey and Lucy Washbourne are in love in spite of the fact that they are on opposite sides in the Civil War. He won't change sides and fight for the South; she is a rebel to the core and won't change sides either. Nevertheless, he tells her: "I'm crazy about you Lucy... I want us to be married some day and live together always." Jeff promises to come back and marry her after the war. She agrees to wait for him.

Think about the realities of marriage and who you would be most likely to consider as a potential husband or wife. Answer the following questions:

Would you marry someone from a different country? Religion? Race? Political Party? Explain why or why not. _____

_____

_____

Rank these factors in choosing a husband or wife in order of importance. 1= most important:

physical beauty _____   religion _____

character _____   feeling "in love" _____

financial stability _____   common interests _____

courtesy _____   physical strength _____

health _____   honesty _____

other _____

Describe your ideal husband or wife.

_____

_____

_____

Now work with a small group to see if you can reach a consensus about what makes an ideal mate. Choose one member to report the results of your discussion to the whole group.

Any Questions?

When you finished reading *Rifles for Watie*, did you have some questions that were left unanswered? Write your questions here.

_____

_____

_____

Work alone or in groups to prepare possible answers for the questions you asked above and those written below. When you finish your predictions, share your ideas with the class.

* Where will Jeff and Lucy live after marrying?

* Will they ever talk about the war?

* What will happen if Jeff meets Heifer Hobbs after the war?

* How many children will Jeff and Lucy have?

* What will happen to Dixie, Jeff's pet?

* Describe a reunion between Jeff and General Blunt.

* How long will it take for Union and Confederate soldiers to become friends again?

* What will Dave Gardner's mother say when she has time to sit down and talk?

* What will Jeff do with his Medal of Honor?

* Will Jeff tell his parents much about the war?

* How will Jeff tell a war story to his son?

* Will Lucy learn to cook well?

* What will Jeff and Lucy's attitudes be toward free Black people?

* Describe a conversation between Jeff and Noah Babbit ten years after the war.

* What will Jeff say to his youngest son who wants to volunteer for service in the Spanish American War?

* How will Lucy describe her first meeting with Jeff to her daughters?

* What wedding gifts are Jeff and Lucy likely to receive?

Book Report Ideas

There are numerous ways to report on a book. After you have finished reading *Rifles for Watie* choose one method of reporting that interests you. It may be a way that your teacher suggests, an idea of your own, or one of the ways below.

- **See What I Read?**

  This report is a visual one. A model of a scene from the story can be created, or a likeness of one or more of the characters from the story can be drawn or sculpted.

- **Time Capsule**

  This report provides people living at a "future" time with the reasons why *Rifles for Watie* is such an outstanding book, and gives these "future" people reasons why it should be read. Make a time capsule-type of design, and neatly print or write your reasons inside the capsule. You may wish to hide your capsule after you have shared it with your classmates. Perhaps one day someone will find it and read *Rifles for Watie* because of what you wrote!

- **Come To Life**

  This report is one that lends itself to a group project. A size-appropriate group prepares a scene from the story for dramatization, acts it out, and relates the significance of the scene to the entire book. Costumes and props will add to the dramatization!

- **Into the Future**

  This report predicts what might happen if *Rifles for Watie* were to continue. It may take the form of a story in narrative or dramatic form, or a visual display.

- **A Letter to the Author**

  In this report, you can write a letter to Mr. Keith. Tell him what you liked about *Rifles for Watie*, and ask him any questions you may have about the writing of the book. You might want to give him some suggestions for a sequel! After your teacher has read it, and you have made your writing the best it can be, send it to him in care of the publishing company.

- **Guess Who or What!**

  This report takes the form of several games of "Twenty Questions." The reporter gives a series of clues about a character from the story in a vague to precise, general to specific order. After all clues have been given, the identity of the mystery character must be deduced. After the character has been guessed, the same reporter presents another "Twenty Questions" about an event in the story.

- **A Character Comes To Life!**

  Suppose one of the characters in *Rifles for Watie* came to life and walked into your home or classroom. This report gives a view of what this character sees, hears, and feels as he or she experiences the world in which you live.

- **Sales Talk**

  This report serves as an advertisement to "sell" *Rifles for Watie* to one or more specific groups. You decide on the group to target and the sales pitch you will use. Include some kind of graphics in your presentation.

- **Coming Attraction!**

  Rifles for Watie is about to be made into a movie and you have been chosen to design the promotional poster. Include the title and author of the book, a listing of the main characters and the contemporary actors who will play them, a drawing of a scene from the book, and a paragraph synopsis of the story.

- **Literary Interview**

  This report is done in pairs. One student will pretend to be a character in the story, steeped completely in the person of his or her character. The other student will play the role of a television or radio interviewer, trying to provide the audience with insights into the character's personality and life. It is the responsibility of the partners to create meaningful questions and appropriate responses.

Find Out More!

Describe three things you read in *Rifles for Watie* that you want to learn more about.

1. _____

2. _____

3. _____

As you read *Rifles for Watie*, you encountered geographical locations, historical events, culturally diverse people, survival techniques, and a variety of animals and plants. To understand the story better and appreciate Harold Keith's craft as a writer, research to find out more about these people, places, and things.

Work in groups to research one or more of the areas you named above, or the areas that you mentioned below. Share your findings with the rest of the class in any appropriate form of oral presentation.

People and Events
* Abraham Lincoln
* Stephen Douglas
* Jefferson Davis
* Bleeding Kansas
* Kansas-Nebraska Act
* Emancipation Proclamation
* Robert E. Lee
* Mexican War
* Rebels
* Yankees
* Slavery

Native Americans

* Cherokees
* Choctaws
* Chickasaws
* Seminoles
* Creeks
* Potowatomie
* Miami

Trees

* history
* oak
* cottonwood
* cedar

Places
* Boggy Depot
* Tahlequah
* Sugar Mound
* Baxter Springs
* Red River
* Canadian River
* Arkansas River
* Ft. Scott
* Ft. Gibson
* Ft. Washita
* Ft. McCullogh
* Honey Springs
* Cane Hill
* North Fork Town
* Perryville

Foraging

* sweet potatoes
* goose
* hog
* hardtack
* pokeberry
* sorghum
* rice
* cornbread
* watermelon
* Confederate "coffee"
* dandelion

Culminating Activity   *Rifles for Watie*

Famous Battles of the Civil War

Directions

1. Divide the class into ten small groups and give each group a different battle from one of the ten battles listed on page 40. Add additional battles if you like.

2. Have each group write a short description of the famous battle. Things to include are the date of the battle, the commanders, number of casualties for both sides, and the results of the battle. Use the Famous Battle form (page 41) for the final draft.

3. When each group has completed its page, assemble the pages into a book, using the artwork from this page on the cover. Title the book "Famous Battles of the Civil War" and display it in the classroom. Have each group present an oral report to the class about its battle. As an extention, have students research famous people of the civil war.

Famous Battles

Directions

Cut out these names of famous battles and give one to each group. They will be used for the "Famous Battles of the Civil War" class book (see page 41).

Antietam MD (Sharpsburg)	**Bull Run** VA (Manassass) first battle
Bull Run VA (Manassass) second battle	**Chancellorsville** VA
Chickamauga GA	**Franklin** TN
Fredericksburg VA	**Gettysburg** PA
Petersburg VA	**Perrysville** KY

Civil War Battle

Unit Test

Matching

Match the character with the description:

1. _____ Shot by raiders   a. Jeff Bussey

2. _____ Indian leader   b. Sgt. Mulholland

3. _____ Union volunteer   c. Stand Watie

4. _____ Professional soldier   d. Captain Clardy

5. _____ Jeff's true love   e. Lucy Washbourne

True or False

Write true or false next to each statement below. On the back of this test paper, explain why each false answer is false.

1. _____ Stand Watie led the Cherokee Mounted Rifles.

2. _____ Jeff became a spy after shooting Clardy.

3. _____ Dave Gardner ran away from the army.

4. _____ Lucy Washbourne served as a Union nurse.

5. _____ Lee Washbourne is shot for spying.

6. _____ Captain Clardy sells rifles to the Union Army.

7. _____ Heifer Hobbs is a Confederate cook.

8. _____ Leemon Jones is a slave who delivers Jeff's report.

9. _____ The Jackmans turn Jeff in for spying.

10. _____ Jeff escaped from Boggy Depot and made it 125 miles on foot to Ft. Gibson.

Short Answer

1. The family that cares for Jeff when he is ill. _____.
2. The state that Jeff is from _____.
3. Jeff and Noah win medals after the battle of _____.
4. Lieutenant Orff carries a Spencer _____.
5. What happened to Clardy at the end of the book? _____.

Essay

1. On the back of this paper, discuss how Jeff is fighting against his own army as well as the rebels.

2. On the back of this paper, describe the role Noah Babbitt and Heifer Hobbs play in Jeff's life.

Response

Explain the meaning of each of these quotations from *Rifles for Watie.*

Chapter 4 " 'I won't change it. My father gave me that name.' "

Chapter 5 " 'You walked sixty miles away from me to enlist and now you come crawlin' back to tell me you're tired of it and that you wanted to come back home. You're in the army.' "

Chapter 7 " 'What's your excuse for being here instead of at the front?... Are you looking for some other widow's eight hundred dollars?' "

Chapter 9 " 'It's me m'am. I brought your cow back.' "

Chapter 10 " 'We call that trip "Trail of Tears" because they have to stop ever' few miles and bury somebody.' "

Chapter 11 " 'Since you freed all the Negroes, we're not even cooking dinner for ourselves...We're all rebels—to the backbone.' "

" 'M'am, you're supposed to milk from the cow's right side, not her left...Why don't you let me milk her for you?' "

Chapter 13 " 'Jimmy, only Jesus is able to save you.' "

Chapter 14 " 'What ye hangin' round these rebel wimmen fer?...Yer sweet on the youngest 'un, ain't ye?' "

Chapter 18 " 'They know all about Clardy havin' Lee Washbourne shot. The whole rebel army is sore about it. Their pickets said the Watie men have sworn that the first Clardy man they capture behind their lines will go before a firin' squad before he can say God with his mouth open.' "

Teacher Note: Choose an appropriate number of quotes for your students.

Conversations

Work in groups to write and perform the conversations that might have occurred in each of the following situations.

* Dave Gardner refuses to go back to the fort after deserting. Jeff is assigned to bring him in. (2 people)

* General Blunt catches 2 soldiers stealing watermelons. (3 people)

* Captain Clardy recognizes Jeff when he first rides up with the Watie men to buy rifles. (3 people)

* Jeff and Lucy discuss their marriage plans, who they will invite, where they will live, etc. (2 people)

* Jeff and Noah Babbitt are reunited 10 years after the war. (2 people)

* Jeff is caught and about to be executed as a spy, but is given a chance to say a few last words. (2 people)

* Lucy politely refuses a proposal of marriage from a rebel soldier. (2 people)

* Jeff meets Heifer Hobbs and Stand Watie 10 years after the war. (3 people)

* Heifer Hobbs and Sam Fields have a heated discussion after discovering that Jeff was, indeed, a spy. (2 people)

* Jeff's parents meet Lucy Washbourne for the first time. (4 people)

* Stand Watie and several white soldiers discuss who is more civilized, Indians or whites. (3 or 4 people)

* Mrs. McCommas sees Jeff while he is hiding from rebels who are hunting him down. (2 people)

* Write and perform one of your own conversation ideas for the characters in *Rifles for Watie.*

Bibliography of Related Reading

Albaugh, William A. *Confederate Edged Weapons.* (Harper, 1960)

Barry, James. P. *Bloody Kansas.* (Franklin Watts, 1972)

Campbell, C.W. *Sequoyah.* (Dillon, 1973)

Carpenter, Allan. *Oklahoma.* (Childrens Press, 1979)

Fradin, Dennis B. *Oklahoma in Words and Pictures.* (Childrens Press, 1981)

Green, Michael D. *The Creeks.* (Chelsea House, 1990)

Hale, Duane K. and Arnell Gibson. *The Chickasaw.* (Chelsea House, 1991)

Hayman, Leroy. *The Road to Fort Sumter.* (Crowell, 1972)

Heinrichs, Ann. *Oklahoma* (Childrens Press, 1989)

Lepthien, Emilie. *The Choctaw.* (Childrens Press, 1987)

       The Cherokee. (Childrens Press, 1985)

Lincoln, President Abraham. "Gettysburg Address," "Second Inaugural Address." (Found in most American history texts)

Perdue, Theda. *The Cherokee.* (Chelsea House, 1989)

Peterson, Harold L. *The Treasury of the Gun.* (Ridge Press, 1962)

Phelan, Mary Kay. *Mr. Lincoln Speaks at Gettysburg.* (Norton, 1966)

Pratt, Fletcher. *The Civil War.* (Doubleday, 1955)

Public Broadcasting System. *The Civil War.* (Film, 1990)

Robertson, James. *Concise Illustrated History of the Civil War.* (Stackpole Books, 1971)

Sterling, Dorothy. *Forever Free: The Story of the Emancipation Proclamation.* (Doubleday, 1963)

Tunis, Edwin. *Weapons: A Pictorial History.* (World Publishing, 1954)

Webb, Robert N. *The Raid on Harper's Ferry.* (Franklin Watts, 1971)

White, William C. and Ruth Write. *Tin Can on a Shingle.* (E.P. Dutton, 1957)

Wiley, Bell I. *The Life of Billy Yank.* (Doubleday, 1971)

       The Life of Johnny Reb. (Bobbs-Merrill, 1962)

Windrow, Martin. *The Civil War Rifleman.* (Franklin Watts, 1985)

Woods, Harold and Geraldine Woods. *The South Central States.* (Franklin Watts, 1984)

Answer Key

Page 10

1. Accept appropriate responses.
2. Southern bushwhackers threatened anti-slavery settlers in Kansas. Border ruffians from Missouri complicated what was to be a simple election under the Kansas-Nebraska Act, to determine the status of slavery in Kansas.
3. Jeff decides to join the Union Army. He is fed up with the bushwhackers.
4. Jefferson Davis is the name of the president of the Confederacy.
5. Captain Clardy resents Jeff's name and his "back talk". As a professional soldier, he despises volunteer officers over him. He's especially bitter about Jefferson Davis, who was elected officer in his place during the Mexican War.
6. Dave deserts the army and goes back home. Jeff talks him into coming back.
7. Accept reasonable answers.
8. Jeff washed pots and kettles, peeled potatoes, and emptied swill after drilling all day.
9. They lie to the guard, sneak under a fence at night.
10. Accept reasonable answers.

Page 13

F	A	C	G	K	H	B	D	L	J	I	E
1820	1838-1839	1846-1848	1854	1855-1860	1859	1860	1861	1862	1863		1865

Page 16

1. Accept appropriate responses.
2. Jimmy Lear is only 14, too young to legally fight, but shows heroism anyway when he drops his drum and picks up a gun.
3. Clardy puts him on all night sentry duty.
4. Clardy killed a widow in Oswatomie and stole her eight hundred dollars. He slipped into her house on a stormy night.
5. Jeff is disappointed because he doesn't get to fight in the battle because he was ordered to the rear to find the quartermaster.
6. Ford Ivey has his leg amputated.
7. Jeff is assigned to bury the dead. He adopts a new dog, Dixie, whose Southern master fell in battle.
8. Clardy blames Confederates. Jeff suspects Clardy because Sparrow knew Clardy was a murderer.
9. Rebel families had their livestock confiscated. Jeff takes Mrs. McCommas' cow back to her in exchange for bread and apple butter.
10. Chief John Ross led the Union Cherokees; Stand Watie, the Confederates. Union home guard Cherokees march barefoot, etc.

Page 19

1. The U.S. Army force marched Indians from Georgia to Oklahoma in the 1830's. Many died on this "trail of tears."
2. Many Cherokees held black slaves.
3. Accept reasonable answers.
4. Accept well-supported answers.

Page 21

1. Accept appropriate responses.
2. 16 year old, pretty daughter of a prosperous rebel Cherokee family in Tahlequah. Jeff is very "moonstruck" from the first time he sees her.
3. They were hostile at first, then show hospitality and feed him after he helps milk their cow.
4. After cannon fire, Jeff's regiment charges the rebels. Jeff and Noah help out with a Union cannon after their charge.
5. Noah Babbitt saves Jeff's life as he is struggling hand to hand.
6. Jimmy is run over by a caisson and IS near death.
7. The town had food and supplies the soldiers wanted: ham, tobacco, shoes, and socks.
8. He salted the back of her calf so the cow would let it nurse. He fought off Union hecklers.

Answer Key *(cont.)*

9. Watie raiders killed Frank, the father, stole all their food, clothing, bedding, and livestock. They also destroyed their field and set fire to the house. Confederates wanted to destroy all Union supplies and force all Union families to live off the fort.
10. Accept all reasonable answers.

Page 23
Group 1
1. More could be killed because several shots could be fired without reloading.
2. There were many bloody battles about whether Kansas would be a free state or a slave state.
3. Gettysburg, PA
4. 1861
5. 1864

Group 2
1. He was a famous Civil War photographer.
2. Soldiers who deserted after being paid to enlist.
3. To become a Union state.
4. Appomattox
5. 1863

Group 3
1. Alabama, Arkansas, Florida, Georgia, Louisiana, Mississippi, North Carolina, South Carolina, Tennessee, Texas, Virginia
2. West Point
3. Disease
4. 1865
5. 9,000,000

Group 4
1. Wooden ships with iron siding
2. The court declared that no Black person could be a U.S. citizen.
3. Jefferson Davis
4. General Sherman
5. 14,754

Page 24
Accept reasonable estimates: 30, 60, 60, 30, 45, 15.
240 miles total.

Page 26
1. Accept appropriate answers.
2. Jeff arranges for Lee Washbourne's body to be sent back to Lucy's family.
3. General Blunt saw Jeff in action at the Battle of Prairie Grove and trusts him. He needs information about Watie.
4. Jeff helps Noah escape from Confederate raiders.
5. Lucy kisses him and tells him she likes him, but she is still a rebel.
6. Bostwick says they are on their way to join Watie's outfit.
7. Bostwick's canteen has real "Yankee coffee."
8. Jeff falls ill and the Jackmans take care of him. He goes to Texas with them.
9. A young slave, Leemon Jones.
10. Accept all reasonable answers.

Answer Key *(cont.)*

Page 31
1. Accept appropriate responses.
2. It would probably prolong the war, giving the South the advantage of greater fire power from fewer soldiers.
3. They are friendly, the food is good, the officers are less formal.
4. He has to hide his feelings, he feels guilty because the rebels are friendly, and he respects them.
5. Captain Clardy is a traitor to the Union because he is selling repeating rifles to the Confederates.
6. Jeff runs away, on foot, from Boggy Depot to Fort Gibson, hiding from the rebels who are tracking him.
7. Jeff tells Lucy he will come back and marry her.
8. Jeff befriends one of the rebel bloodhounds sent to find him.
9. His horse and the dog.
10. Accept reasonable answers.

Page 33
1. Heifer takes care of Jeff when he is sick, gives him a new horse, defends him against accusations of spying.
2. Stand Watie was a quiet, courteous, and dignified old man.
3. The Jackmans show hospitality to Jeff, who is charmed by girls. They are intelligent, respectable, Christian people. Dark-complected Cherokee.
4. Lucy is a dark-complected Cherokee from a prosperous, courteous, and hospitable family. She is proud, saucy, and completely charms Jeff; helpless with milking.
5. Hooley befriends Jeff, explains Indian ways; Jeff helps him out by sharing a horse after Hooley is wounded at Pheasant Bluff.

Page 34
They built it fifteen years before I was born. They sure did do something. It stands there in the woods pointing its spire up towards heaven. Every time I pass it, I feel kind of reverent.
You all can eat with our mess here.
Sam, You're addled. What else does the boy have to do today to prove himself to you, tote you on his back all the way from Honey Springs to the Red River.
Hop in there and crawl between the covers.
That Miss Pat has done it again. She is never going to learn to walk gracefully, like a lady.
They fixed you a pallet in the back of one of the wagons.

Page 42
Matching: 1)b 2)c 3)a 4)d 5)e
True or False
1. True
2. False; Jeff never shoots Clardy.
3. True
4. False; Lucy is a rebel Cherokee.
5. True
6. False; Clardy, a traitor to his Union, sells rifles to the rebels.
7. True
8. True
9. False; the Jackman's show hospitality while Jeff is ill.
10. True
Short Answer
1. Jackmans
2. Kansas
3. Prairie Grove
4. repeating rifle
5. He is stabbed to death.
Essay
1. Accept appropriate responses. Jeff resists military discipline and cruelty from Captain Clardy; he hates the suffering his own army causes civilians.
2. Accept appropriate responses. Noah is an older man that takes care of the younger Jeff in the Union army. Heifer plays the same role when Jeff is in the Cherokee rebel cavalry.

Page 43
Accept all reasonable and well-supported answers.

Page 44
Perform the conversation in class. Ask students to respond to the conversations in several different ways, such as, "Are the conversations realistic?" or, "Do the words the characters say match their personalities?"